Healthy Living

Keeping Clean at Home

By Katlin Sarantou

I clean the table.

I clean the dishes.

I clean the counter.

I clean the windows.

I clean the floor.

I clean the toys.

I clean the shelves.

I clean the bed.

I clean the steps.

I clean the dog.

I clean the bathtub.

I clean the sink.

Word List

clean
table
dishes
counter
windows
floor
toys
shelves
bed
steps
dog
bathtub
sink

48 Words

I clean the table.
I clean the dishes.
I clean the counter.
I clean the windows.
I clean the floor.
I clean the toys.
I clean the shelves.
I clean the bed.
I clean the steps.
I clean the dog.
I clean the bathtub.
I clean the sink.

Published in the United States of America by Cherry Lake Publishing
Ann Arbor, Michigan
www.cherrylakepublishing.com

Photo Credits: ©DGLimagesFront/shutterstock.com, front cover; ©MIA Studio/Shutterstock.com, 1; ©Maria Evseyeva/Shutterstock.com, 2; ©giuseppelombardo/Shutterstock.com, 3; ©Daniel Jedzura/Shutterstock.com, 4; ©ZouZou/Shutterstock.com, 5; ©Elizaveta Galitckaia/Shutterstock.com, 6; ©PIGAMA/Shutterstock.com, 7; ©LightField Studios/Shutterstock.com, 8; ©Rawpixel.com/Shutterstock.com, 9; ©FamVeld/Shutterstock.com, 10; ©Glynsimages2013/Shutterstock.com, 11; ©hanapon1002/Shutterstock.com, 12; ©DGLimages/Shutterstock.com, 13; ©sunabesyou/Shutterstock.com, 15, back cover

Cherry Blossom Press is an imprint of Cherry Lake Publishing.

Library of Congress Cataloging-in-Publication Data

Names: Sarantou, Katlin, author.
Title: Keeping clean at home / Katlin Sarantou.
Description: Ann Arbor, Michigan : Cherry Lake Publishing, [2020] | Series: Healthy living | Audience: Grades K-1. | Summary: "Learn how you can help keep your home clean. The book utilizes social emotional based text to get children comfortable with reading, and uses the Whole Language approach to literacy, a combination of sight words and repetition builds recognition and confidence. Bold, colorful photographs correlate directly to text to help guide readers through the book"– Provided by publisher.
Identifiers: LCCN 2019034076 (print) | LCCN 2019034077 (ebook) | ISBN 9781534160989 (paperback) | ISBN 9781534159839 (pdf) | ISBN 9781534162136 (ebook)
Subjects: LCSH: House cleaning–Juvenile literature. | Hygiene–Juvenile literature. | Readers (Elementary)
Classification: LCC TX324 .S2257 2020 (print) | LCC TX324 (ebook) | DDC 648/.5–dc23
LC record available at https://lccn.loc.gov/2019034076
LC ebook record available at https://lccn.loc.gov/2019034077

Printed in the United States of America
Corporate Graphics

Cherry Blossom Press